First Edition Published 2000

Shih, Seng, Dalai, 1929-
          The Way: Neo Ch'an Book of Prayers
Includes index.
ISBN 0-9683504-5-3

     1. Prayers   I. Title.
BL560.S536 2000   291.4'33   C00-900523-4

Jacket design by K. Laninga
Artwork graciously painted by Alex Fong

Published by:
Golden Bell Publishing House Inc.
P.O. Box 2680, Grand Forks, B.C. Canada V0H1H0
www.goldenbellhouse.com

The Way

The Neo Ch'an Temple
Book
of
Prayers

His Holiness
The Dalai Seng Shih
of the Neo Ch'an Buddhist Temple

Foreword

As modern man traveled the heavens, he was exalted by the extension of his realm. When he saw the earth floating beneath him, he was captured by the fear of losing it; thus, when he returned to earth, he discovered that very Heaven, which his intellect had long since annulled. Since we accept that we are all children of one Creator, or that power which creates, do we struggle with the idea of a beginning and an end to all things. The human intellect has, within its structure, the ability to search, identify and embellish thought to such a degree that it equals the boundless regions of the universe, which is constantly engulfed in rebirth and destruction. If God, indeed, created man, who then created Him?

As our mind is tied to life and life to time, futility lies in the search for vanished shadows. Does man truly preach God's words or does inspiration invite them? Does man divide the heavens of this one God by making claims that his God is the only true one? Is the vindictiveness of wisdom and revenge a blessing? The mind of the fanatic will, if given a chance, erase his unwanted god from the space the heavens hold, leading his own god, as well, toward the path of destruction. Therefore, if the spirit of God does not live within our minds, the greatest and most spacious heaven will not be able to sustain him.

Civilization afforded us the tools with which to control our emotions; but modern day man is being governed by forces which begin to exploit them once again. Man is given the choice for betterment which lies in equal measure within fear and reason. However, reason excites little popularity and will, therefore, remain a part of the few rather than with the many. Yet, if inspiration could be made the sun in our lives, religion and reason combined, when reformed within the glory of democratic thought, could then unite again within the formulation of a universal message; and once more save all people while they are still living, dispersing the shadow the nuclear age has cast upon mankind.

Faith accepts change only when it comes from man being alive - from living man: The dead man cannot change his ways any longer.

-His Holiness,
the Dalai Seng Shih of the
Neo Ch'an Buddhist Temple

His Holiness The Dalai Seng Shih

His Holiness, the Dalai Seng Shih

The Dalai Seng Shih is the founder of the Neo Ch'an Buddhist Temple. Believing in Buddha's teachings regarding the striving for purity of mind and body but also believing in the existence of a creative power which he felt confronts man everywhere, He elected to found this new form of Buddhism on the basis of Neo Ch'an thought. Neo, meaning of course new and Ch'an or Zen referring to enlightenment allows for a living philosophy not bound by the stringency of the past. The faith thus embraces all religions, which find solace in God, and recognizes this unknown entity as being the creative force in the universe. Thus there are Neo Ch'an Buddhists, Neo Ch'an Jews, Neo Ch'an Catholics, Neo Ch'an Moslems, Neo Ch'an Christians.

Leaving a war torn Europe, His Holiness began a new life in North America, teaching, lecturing, writing, always emphasizing purity of mind and body in a realistic and modern way. Having witnessed man at his best and definitely at his worst, especially in wartime, his experiences have provided him with a tremendous wisdom for which all those who have been his students are very grateful for he shares his insight, his very special wisdom and his compassion with us all so that we may embrace his philosophy and continue on into the future to make a better world for all to live in. Stressing always independency of thought, freedom of control of the mind by others, He liberates us yet cautions us to maintain a respect for that which is around us and that which has created us and to maintain that unwritten code throughout our lives. For this, we His followers, are forever grateful.

Most Gracious Reverend, Nanlao

The Way

The Neo Ch'an Temple
Book
of
Prayers

His Holiness
The Dalai Seng Shih
of the Neo Ch'an Buddhist Temple

The Way
Neo Ch'an Temple
Book of Daily Prayers

INDEX

I........ The Light
II...... To Seek
III..... The Spirit
IV..... To Love
V...... To Look Within
VI..... To be Free
VII.... To Conquer Evil
VIII... To Carry Its Light
IX..... Wisdom
X....... The Greatest Gift
XI...... Truth
XII.... Temptation
XIII... The Great Spirit
XIV... The Enemy
XV..... The Shrine

XVI...... Eternity
XVII.... The Measurement
XVIIII.. Cannot Fail
XIX...... The Past
XX...... The Knights of Heaven
XXI..... In Praise of Thee
XXII..... The Future
XXIII... To Pray
XXIV... The Centre
XXV.... Purpose
XXVI... Balance
XVII.... The Noble Path
XXVIII. Right Thought
XXIX.... Through the Buddha
XXX.... Mercy of the Buddha
XXXI.... Defending the Good

The Neo Ch'an Temple

BookofPrayers

I. The Light

Greatest spirit, Lord or shining sun,
falling rain or rising mist,
let my soul recover in Thy presence
as I see the flame of this candle
reach to Heaven.

May my struggle be worth my promise
so I can find the light.

- Amen

II. To Seek

As the flame of my candle, which I lit
    to find the light where it was missing,
            reaches up,
it reminds me to search for more light
as I find it in the presence of a sunrise.

As my Lord allows me to worship
    in any temple where there is His presence,
may my soul be aware that I seek His love,
            never His fear.

                        - Amen

III. The Spirit

I am here. There is no candle with me
  but as sure as there is life, its light,
the light of this candle, will shine in my soul
because life everlasting has the touch of dew
as well as it has the touch of fire.
The living spirit,
  which must be somewhere residing,
this spirit I call God, and I shall listen
to the many names mankind has given
       unto Him.
Let no man tell you that you must shudder
before Him, this spirit,
  His spirit, yours and mine.
Man tells that we must have fear of this spirit
  so man can achieve power over others
where God's spirit should rightfully be.
His teachings can never be to fear Him.
How then can we approach
  such universal power, if we are already
afraid of that which has created us
  in the first place?
And thus, I shall endure in any temple
  which accepts my prayer in His glory.
       -Amen

IV. To Love

If I learn to worship the wind,
   I will also feel the silence of its streaming air
   when it thunders past me,
   because I am a human being
   and can think the opposite.
Much glory lies then not only in the heavens
   but also here where I dwell.
As I enrich my soul, I will gain strength
   to inspire others
   and learn not of the cheap kind of love
   but the one which makes a man taller
   and a woman more free
   than Nature can, herself, imagine.

- Amen

V. To Look Within

It is struggle alone which makes the stars shine,
  passing their light through measureless time
  to adorn the Heaven above me.

As too many say that there is no God,
  I will surrender my thoughts and look
  at the candle I lit and I will see
  that it comes alive with His spirit.

It was in the power of the Creator
  to tell and give Himself a body;
yet, I cannot find it,
  until I learn to look into my soul
for here, alone, will I see a future
  resting in a glorious struggle
  as all life functions,
  always like the flame of my candle
    reaching for more light.

-    Amen

VI. To be Free

As I have folded my hands,
   I feel the warmth of their touch
   uplifting my energy from within
      to my palms.

As I bow my head as a free person
   before this shrine,
I am taught also to raise it here in pride,
   to be a human being
   free of the enslavement of any thought
just reaching out to where the heavens are
to better feel the spirit of my Creator -
and as I part my hands
and let my arms reach into Heaven,
it is as if to touch the souls
of all those who love God
   not in fear but in glory.

I must believe that I am as devoted to God
   if my arms reach out to Him
as the very man who falls on his face
before this shrine.

           -Amen

VII. To Conquer Evil

All souls who reach to Heaven
   find Allah, God and even Jehovah,
and yet, they are taught to stray
and exclude the same souls
who find a different path to Him.
Who then is at error: God or man?

God, Himself, created a vast space
   that heavens should not collide; yet they do.
Since God made man,
He also must have had a maker Himself.
We learn this creative power seldom errs
and find that man does err much more often.

May I learn to bring man together:
   may my spirit have the courage
to defend peace with wisdom.

It is not the weapon
   which will win any war:
it is the human spirit
which can master it-
   start it, end it
and dissolve its evil.

May I learn of the evil spirits in men
   who smile and praise
and tell that they are of Heaven,
and alone hold the key to its gate.

I rather learn to pray to the stone;
for the stone is kind and only rolls
if disturbed from where it rested.

- Amen

VIII. To Carry Its Light

I have learned to pray rather for others
   so I may not think too much about myself.
Since all souls in my Temple pray for others,
we shall become of each other
  through such spirit alone.
Love is not idle and aimless,
  sitting and wasting away the days
  the Lord offered to me.
Love is the struggle to find the way,
  not to lose it; and to have faith in my mind,
  to treat this mind right and not to poison it;
  to challenge it within the frame of kindness,
  encouraging it if it falters;
and to uplift this, my spirit, before this shrine
so I may gain strength and the power to walk
  more free than when I came.

As I quiet the flame of my candle,
I, as well, shall be calm
and carry its light within me.
                   - Amen

IX. Wisdom

I do not have to call for any Buddha.
The will toward wisdom does not
    lie within him:
it is resting with me.
If this is not the temple of my choice,
    I shall better appreciate its dome,
    for my Lord is yours
    and always was.

Where then lies Heaven
    and why is man so fearful
    to see it everywhere?

My soul, even if deprived,
    shall win over all temptations,
    because a good mind
    is one which is free of errors.
I shall arrive at a day
    when my errors are much less
    than they were yesterday.

- Amen

X. The Greatest Gift

On the day on which I was born,
   there was light as well as darkness
   surrounding me.
I was listening to the sounds of life.
I did not as yet know of the sound
   of my own heartbeat.
I can see and hear and feel all life.
I can walk and run,
   climb and even fly,
or I may have lost all these gifts of Heaven;
yet, amongst my people,
   I am free and alive
and am a part of them all.

May the Lord never take those away from me
   who worship in silence,
   refusing the beat of a drum,
but still praise the light of my candle.
              - Amen

XI. Truth

If you know about truth,
      tell me of it.

If not,
      I shall search with you, together,
        in order to find it.

          - Amen

XII. Temptation

Having erred may not please my scripture,
   nor does it enhance this prayer,
but it challenges my soul so much so
that my temptations shall rise
into the light of the sun
so that the light coming from that source
   may burn them.

- Amen

XIII. The Great Spirit

Oh yes, let me pray to the Great Spirit,
   the power that I cannot reach
without thought;
   for right thought, in itself, is the foundation,
      the spark of the spirit.

There are small and great spirits.
All the wealth on earth and even in Heaven
   ties into the human spirit.
May the Great Spirit protect me
from many losses,
         wrong wealth and wrong friends.

Yet, the loss of my spirit
 will render futile the powers of love
 which reside in the Great Spirit,
 the spirit above me,
 the one which lives behind things,
 the one that is permanent
 as it lives in water and rivers,
 fields and meadows,
 mountains and clouds.

I ask the Great Spirit to unite all peoples
 who struggle to find
 an everlasting solution
 for all spirits who are troubled.

May the Great Spirit teach me true values,
 the ones which unite me
  with the rest of all people.

- Amen

XIV. The Enemy

I have lit the candle and am praying
   that my enemies may fall
before they are able to destroy my land.

But, I shall not deprive an enemy
   who in honour errs
and shall rather lift him from his wounds
   and carry him into my Temple,
showing him that his Lord
   was all along my Lord.

I shall pray for him
   and return him to his people,
   telling them that his God
    was not at fault,
but that the message he brought,
  sent by his messenger,
had not been understood.

It is not for me to love an enemy
   but to secure that his error may match mine;
since, war, conflict in itself,
   shows not the error of only one
   but the errors of all.

      - Amen

XV. The Shrine

Having been homeless brethren and sisters
   and having struggled for time unending,
it is I who sees the Temple in the image
   of goodness in my mind.
I see the land on which I may tread
   and I shall draw courage from it
      as I breathe the air high above the valley.

I may wait for the stars to come and yet,
   I may arrive at the shrine
   when the day is still in the making
and find that my shrine
      stands for all of mankind.

The sanctum stands for me
   and blesses the quietness around
as I walk and rest and dream.

And even if I do not utter one word
   but remain silent,
my thoughts become a prayer,
one which does not have to be spoken aloud;
yet, the great spirit of God will listen
   with greater trust and guide me just as surely.
In silence rests trust,
   in noise the act of boasting,
        a path opposing peace.

As my spirit walks over this land,
it shall meet the many others who linger here,
and it shall rest with the breeze
of the many spirits who choose to remain.

- Amen

XVI. Eternity

Five butterflies, or even six, maybe a dozen
   all hover round my quiet place.
The bees are flying slow as darkness sets in,
and as I turn my head
back to the sleeping shrine
and see its shadow fading slowly with the sun,
     all open blossoms close.

But then, one seed falls from a tree nearby,
spiralling to the soil, dying into new life
as does man follow in like fashion,
   never really dying
   always truly living
as long as the spirit of the Temple
   stays quiet within our minds.

- Amen

XVII. The Measurement

There is a living heaven within the feelings
    of a heart as it struggles.
There is little feeling in the heart
    that does not know of struggle,
and sees struggle only in the effort for gain.

A good soul is not necessarily measured
    by the power of feeling,
but much more so
    by the strength to overcome feelings.
And most of all:
    emotions are feelings
    which should never be allowed
        to corrupt one's mind.

- Amen

XVIII. I Cannot Fail

As my struggle goes with me,
I have brought it to this shrine
and am thus opposing the sanctuary of peace.
Since, I carry anger in my heart,
I shall have to learn to suspend it here
while I pray,
to speak to my soul within
    which seems to listen best
whenever it is near the shrine.

As I was taught to struggle on in patience,
    did I adhere to the advice
    of those who lived ahead of me,
the ones who had already experienced my lot.
But, since, in all of my endeavours,
    I have only lost,
    I do not know of victory.
I have never seen the reward
    for my struggle.

In the presence of silence,
  I sense relief as I breathe calmly;
and as the wind strikes the high trees,
  their branches begin to sing to me
  of the warriors who struggled on
  never seeing victory until the sun
  vanished from the sky.

But now, I see.
For in the shadow
  all along rested the strength of the light
  which I failed to sense.
Praying now in the shadow, therefore,
  the remnants of light
must rest in your shadow,
and having learned of this secret,
  my soul will shine in glory.
I now know that all the losses I counted
  were victories all along.

It is, therefore, that I cannot fail
    because the shadows of this shrine
    are like the shadows of its candles
    when their flames mirror my thoughts
        back to me.

It is then when life surpasses all,
    when the shade begins to glow
because I do not desert my struggle,
    the effort which allows me
    to share my spirit
    with all those souls
    who battle on,
    forward in time.

                -    Amen

XIX. The Past

As time moves,
   the past will not go from us
but be of time,
   behind us.
Therefore, all our failures
   are of that past,
meaning now,
   that victory
   can only lie ahead.

Why then abandon
   our struggle:
for the victories to come
will rise from the shadows
   of our past
   as the phoenix did
   when climbing out of the ashes
to leave his past as well.

- Amen

XX. Knights of Heaven

I am the Knight of Heaven
   and this is the shrine,
   yours and mine, to prove it.
The many altars which truly worship God
   are united under this one roof;
for my Temple has become
   the Temple of all,
since it does not quarrel with those
   who say that they believe.

Such vision embraces all differences
   and truly speaks of unison,
a unity of purpose in which no agitator
   can find his cause for action.
The greatness of spiritual love
   lies in such offering
which allows all to worship everywhere
without the attempt or faintest idea
that they should abandon their faith
   for a better one; for, no faith
can serve us which betrays the holiness
of conduct that lies in your wishing
   to remain with your vision of God.
A Knight of Heaven is a worshipping being

who can easily pray in any duly ordained
   house of the Lord and thus,
   sanctify it with his presence.
A Knight of Heaven is a missionary to all
   the teachings which share in the glory of God.
And a Knight of Heaven is a human being
who lives by a code of reason,
so that error may solve itself
through a discourse amongst those who try to
find all that which they have in common
   and lessen all that which divides them.
Such a faith and such a gesture in faith
   allows all people to stay
   with their personal God,
   the one who purifies His and our soul,
elevates our hearts and cleanses our spirits,
giving human dignity to the beams which hold
such a roof, crowning civility, honour and trust,
   love and forgiveness and, above all, justice
   against those who dare to destroy
   this Gate of Heaven.
May no state of affairs allow otherwise;
for, if it does, nobility and the holiness
which rests in the most feeble state of life
   will have been lost forever.

                              - Amen

XXI. In Praise of Thee

Green grass, white snow, blue Heaven,
   the oceans and the deserts too,
'tis that which God has given
for me, for them and even you.

The rain, the sun, the storm which screams,
   the thunder and the lightning's flash,
like hate and cruelty, like love and dreams'
indifference to calm and rash.

And as the sun still rises after dark,
   and while the fire dies
    when it exhausts its flame,
the angels still will praise the lark,
though nothing ever can remain.

And as my prayer speaks of life, it praises Thee,
   the God whom man has found in many faces,
returning all of that which raises me
into a million humble graces.

Placing my soul into my faith,
   I try to grasp the wonder
of all that moves and which
   surrounds life's story:
green grass, white snow,
   blue Heaven yonder,
how love and hate all rest
   in God's almighty glory.

Wide oceans span our time
   and speak of unknown measures,
of distances which seem
   to change the thoughts of man
as time has welded space
   into the closeness of its treasures
which love alone will promise that it can.

- Amen

XXII. The Future

The falling leaves have long since gone which marked
        the ground in splend'rous charm.
The lost ones drift now with the flying snow whose veils
        of icy dust do touch upon our window sill
on which the laughter of forgotten days was leaning
        alike the dreams do rest within the hopeful mind.
Oh may our Lord well cover all the days which passed us by
        and carry them into our hearts to cause no harm.
May all the ones who travelled in our rows
        be free of fear the icy winds instill.
And most of all, may we unite to better our days,
        the times which passed, forget our pain,
because the future has, as struggle goes,
        its own decisive will.
It is the only part of time which can arrange for betterment
        so that our previous hurts were not in vain.

- Amen

XXIII. To Pray

The words of Almighty God
   are being spoken in many tongues
and are as colourful as the flowers
   on this mountain meadow.
They come and go with the seasons of life.
As I pray here before this altar,
   I see my brethren kneeling
and touching the ground
in praise of the Lord,
while I keep on standing
bending only one knee.
Yet, my heart is filled with the same joys of Heaven.
I kneel before the shrine of God
   and not before the powers of man,
   and I fear not God, but I do see fear
   in the faces of many of my brethren.
How is it then that the living masters can tell
   that I have to die for a cause
while they keep on living,
 speaking of the orders to sacrifice
 as if God, Himself,
had ordered that the life He gave
 should so easily be discarded?
The great wisdom of life everlasting lives
in the spirit of the Creator.

Does not the wingbeat of the robin sing of Heaven
   and does not the cry of the wolf speak
   of loneliness in one and the same
   span of a heartbeat?
Does Heaven truly not live on earth
before my spirit passes?
The shrine on this mountain
   and the altar in my distant home
are filled with such a heartbeat,
because the wisdom of life
sails in the clouds above and fills my heart
   with the spirits of man as he struggles to find.
Let us not miss each other's strides, oh my Lord,
as we walk on the road to enrich our lives
with the peace of Heaven which roams above us
   and rings in the bells
   and the callers of God,
reminding us that prayer
may ease the burdens of life
which stem mainly from our inflicted errors.

-     Amen

XXIV. The Centre

The sun has set
  and the birds do not sing any longer.
But out here, unlike in the gilded halls
  of a palace, moves the spirit of life,
  God everlasting.
His breath touches the treetops
  high above me,
and I can hear the words of the Lord
  as His voice fades and swells
  with each breath of wind;
and so tells the wind:
  Beware of the men who speak in My name
  and praise Me and tell you
  that you are lesser and
  have to dwell in My shadow.
  All such souls who lead men onward
  in the fear of Me,
    are not hailing
    the joy of life
    as I have given it to all.
  It is not the blind faith
  which I have created
  as I made the horizon well rounded.

Let your thoughts remain as well rounded
as that horizon
and believe in thoughts
that provoke reason, not fear,
and learn that fear alone
will close the book of life
which I have written
and wish to remain open
so that hope may never cease
to fill the hearts of those who are lonesome.
You will find Me dwelling in every form of life,
reflecting your soul until your spirit returns
to the great cycle of which I always
have been the centre.
Therefore, if your spirit is with Me,
it will remain of that centre
until the return of time
because I am that measure.

- Amen

XXV. 𝔓urpose

Since I have seen the sun rise
   and heard the birds sing,
many days have passed.
But, having you, almighty God, within me,
   having heard your soul
   in the songs of the birds,
and having met your eye
   with the rising of the sun,
I humble myself in happiness.

I have read the words of the Buddha,
the soul who has shown me the path
   towards commitment,
that I am not worshipping
   an aimless stone
but rather see through it
as your beneficial thoughts do
when they read my mind.

Not being a heathen,
I place no value
on what man has shaped
other than that which he has created
for the glory to aid my soul
to envision you, almighty God,
as you must be,
   tranquil and supreme
   free of anger,
when I fold my hands.

I shall serve through you
   with my brethren and sisters
to find the deserving ones,
the ones who will not chatter
   in idle talk
bypassing your light
   which shines upon us
when we least expect it.

- Amen

XXVI. Balance

As there is sunshine and darkness
surrounding us,
   there is also warmth and coldness
and the ones who are deprived of seeing
   will still feel the warmth of light
and will know and believe that it exists.

Then, there are the few who can see
but are deprived of their senses
   in different ways.
Their eyes can perceive beauty
   but their souls are not receptive to it,
and they praise loudness and turmoil
   without their souls having felt
   the blessing of silence.

To them, happiness derives
   from within the chaos they are creating
      to deceive their souls.

Since, there should be joy and happiness
      as there is light and darkness,
      within the balance of a day,
      as nature offers thunder and fire,
should there remain the highs
      and the lows of life
within the bounds
      of such a God-like balance
which blesses and crowns
      the mind of man
if it is taught to reason.

May the Almighty then teach us
to balance a happiness when it overflows
  and not become like the lake
  which leaves its shores
  to drown the meadows.

May there be balanced activity
  in mind and body
and guidance from above and within us
that loyalty remains free of one-sidedness
so fanaticism may not spoil
the efforts of rationality,
        the most precious gift
        so uniquely granted by God
          to man alone.

        - Amen

XXVII. The Noble Path

As I set my foot and stride ahead with temperance,
shall I observe the steps of my fellow travellers
   and enjoy the gaining of distance,
especially when accompanied
   by my brethren in faith.

I shall bless the ones whose temples
   are crossing my path,
   shining with their gilded structures,
   their gables forged high against the heavens.
I shall practice equally as much
   and maybe more often rest
   at places which show less gold
   but true kindness, where the water runs
   in quiet cascades into the whirlpool of dreams.

I shall not fear the great power from Heaven
and only bow alike a servant bows to his master.

What a treacherous path it must be
if one's head may not lift up against the sky
from whence all life has taken its strength.

I shall not have to fear any wrath of God,
my soul being embellished by the beauty
I seek to place on the most barren of ground.

Since it has been here before my time,
I shall tread with great care upon it,
and let my mind plant the trees
and colours for future days.

Such thought will evoke right speech
and evolve into good conduct between myself
    and the most innate object.

My livelihood may depend
on the kindness of others but so also
shall my effort prove to them
    that I am worthy of theirs.

With mindfulness and concentration of mind
shall I arrive at a state
in which even the hostile ones sense
that I am a child of the universe
which God offers to all
    who are wishing to seek,
    learning to find,
    and willing to announce.

                -Amen

XXVIII. Right Thought

As I see the white light break into colours
  beneath the petals of an orchid,
does the obscure
  turn into the obvious.

The dew on the grass stem,
  fractured by light,
proclaims a division of white,
  separating it into colours.

It is here where Nature shows its courage
        for all to see,
that the blending of colours
        and their separation,
at one and the same time,
produce that of which no life
can be without forever.

The deepest sea allows life to flourish,
because light, even if it is not noticed,
is somewhere feeding its content.

With the willingness of Almighty God then,
    has light coloured its being
    and given living men,
    each to their own,
    a touch of His colours
    that they learn to behave
    alike the light beam
    which touches upon the sparkling dew,
    blending the neutral
    with the ordainment of colour.
For many thousand years
    the white beam was thought
to have only the property of one colour, until,
  by inspiration and by a spark of genius,
its fragmentation revealed the errors
  man had sustained for a millennium,
engraving hardship into the souls
  and upon the bodies of his kind.

May I, therefore, be blessed with the gift
to search for right thought,
        the right vision of mind
        which even follows me
into the abyss of darkness
where hate and ignorance fester
        to recruit their mercenaries.

May my soul flow into the heart
        of my fellow travellers
and cause them to follow my spirit
        to the point
where the light leaves the heavens:
truly a place from which truth alone
can be channelled,
        most holy in nature.

                - Amen.

XXIX. Through the Buddha

Through thy sublime body
        do I perceive the universe,
your eternal stone carved out into a symbol
        of the vision of God,
the creative power behind all.

As my prayer reaches the stone,
        so embalmed by man's spirit
as to envision
the most elevated forces of creation,
does it penetrate it to reflect upon my soul.

If the image of a stone
        can truly elevate my spirit,
it must be the image
        of the most sanctified ideal
        which reaches my heart.

Here, my mind understands all that
        which man can relate to,
since, I can see your face and even touch
        your body made out of stone.

It is my soul which can breathe life
        into all that which
        appears to be lifeless
        and treat the stone
as well as the gilded metal
with the same consideration of love.
Yet, somewhere, I seem to fail
        to treat my own soul
as kindly as I am able
to treat the sculptured body
        of your image before me.

But, as I have raised my arms
and after I have made my reverence
        three times over,
I shall sense the reflection
        coming from your innate body.
For the stone
        seems now to reflect
as it transmits my spirit
into the unknown regions of Heaven.

My trying hours shall end
as I receive the reflection
from your image
        which does not speak
but offers a quiet reign
        over all that
        which I cannot grasp.

Ending my prayer,
        I send my thoughts
        into Heaven
that my struggle here
        may ease the burden
which was placed upon me
        by the changing moments
of which my day consisted.

May I bless the stone, then,
        which shows the mirage of hope.
Not worshipping it,
        I still may reach the Almighty
and all the souls will come forth
        from whence they were hidden
        to aid me,
without that I have to utter a word
        to all those who proclaim,
but never have knowledge of,
        love's universal atonement.
                        - Amen

XXX. Mercy of the Buddha

I have returned
       from the busy roads of the day
       just as I began the day,
       following the night
       which was to give me rest,
so that I may well accomplish my tasks
amidst my fellowman.

As the stream of life forges our path,
       strong and willful,
demanding with its swiftness of motion,
am I passing the ones
       who seem to cast no shadow,
       as the light never touches them.

Forgotten thus,
       they see no hope
       and are filled with envy,
       despair and more often so,
       showing aggression.

May my soul extend its rays
        into their minds
and teach them
        the truth of blessingful peace
        by way of my actions.

I shall speak with kindness
        to those who cannot see or touch,
        nor hear or feel
and speak of hope
        in the ways in which
        I am being taught.

I shall give happily to those in need
        and search with others
        to aid them
        in their struggle.
I shall guard my soul
        against those who deceive
and beg mercy for gain from me,
depriving so, the many
        more deserving of mercy.

How less redeeming
         would be my deed
         to aid the ones
         not lacking at all,
their desire building
         on the gift of my kindness
         to further their greed?

No words in the vellums of scriptures
         should speak of mercy alone
without that one
         can see and feel
         that a soul is seeking redemption.
For a person showing no conscience
         is alike evil
         proclaiming the good.

                  -Amen

XXXI. Defending the Good

The good, in its design,
        reflects the mirror of peace
        which is strongly framed
        by light and shadows.

As the absence of shadows
        does not tell
        of the departure of light,
may the soul appearing so empty,
still hide the glory of Heaven.

As the one-sided forces
        in Nature's own circles
        imbalance the heavens,
        crushing the earth
        when its tensions compound,
does man's will
destroy his most splendid achievements,
        when devoid of reason.

The churches and temples,
the domes and the gables
      of the Holy shrines
which were blessed
      by the wisdom
      of the ancient,
are crumbling,
while one prophet
diminishes the achievements
      of the other.

It can never be
      in the design of the universe
      and its Almighty Creator, God,
      governing all,
to dwell on the petty gamble of man,
praising the Lord in such a way
that common destruction arises.

If the torch is being lit,
  inflaming the halls of worship
  or leading its people
  away into capture,
if the forces of evil
proclaim such a day as fulfilment,
may I have the strength
  to unite with those
who have the courage to oppose
such insulting flames
  of hate's own consumption.

The halo of my God,
  resting in my soul
  on the stonework
  of the image of Buddha,
will have the strength
to give light
  to my innermost courage,
to rather seek death
  than see my brethren enslaved.

For all the evil in men,
   they fear the courage of the noble
which reigns on forever,
      restoring lost hope
      for the souls of my soul
which will endure long after
      all light has elapsed
to shine then brightly,
      replacing the sun.

- Amen

If you are interested in information on
the Neo Ch'an Buddhist Temple
or the Neo Ch'an philosophy

you may contact the Temple by:

E-mail direct: neochan@sunshinecable.com

Through our website: www.neochan.com

Or by mail to:

**Neo Ch'an Buddhist Temple
P.O. Box 2680
Grand Forks, B.C.
Canada V0H 1H0**